Yahia Hesham

GOODNIGHT WORLD: A TOUR OF THE EARTH'S WONDERS

Yahia Hesham

GOODNIGHT WORLD: A TOUR OF THE EARTH'S WONDERS

TABLE OF CONTENTS

- Explore the wonders of the ocean and the creatures that live within it, such as whales, dolphins, and seahorses.

- Discuss the importance of sea conservation and the need for humans to protect marine life.

Chapter 4: Goodnight to the Forests

- Discuss the beauty and importance of the world's forests, including the animals that call it their home.

- Introduce the concept of deforestation and the need for reforestation to protect wildlife habitats.

Chapter 5: Goodnight to the Animals

- Explore the diversity of the world's animals, including endangered species and the importance of conservation.

- Discuss the significance of animal symbolism in different cultures.

Chapter 6: Goodnight to the Flowers

- Discuss the beauty of flowers and their cultural meanings and uses, such as in medicine and perfumes.

- Introduce the concept of gardening and the importance of conservation of natural resources.

Chapter 7: Conclusion

- Recap the tour of the world's wonders that was shared in the book.

- Reinforce the importance of taking care of the Earth and appreciating the beauty of the world around us even at bedtime.

INTRODUCTION

Are you ready for a journey through the Earth's amazing wonders? This book is all about saying goodnight to some of the beautiful things that make our world special. We'll explore the significance of the sunset, stars, seas, forests, animals, and flowers, and why it's so important to take care of them.

Have you ever noticed how the sky changes color when the sun sets? We'll talk about why this happens and how different cultures have special ways of saying goodbye to the sun. We'll also discover the magic of stargazing and the significance of constellations in various cultures.

Next, we'll dive into the ocean and learn about the many creatures that call it home, from whales and dolphins to seahorses and crabs. We'll also talk about the importance of taking care of our oceans and how we can work to protect marine life.

Forests are another important part of our Earth's wonders. They are home to many animals such as bears, snakes, and birds. But unfortunately, trees are being cut down faster than they can grow back. We'll learn about the harm caused by deforestation and how we can help preserve forests and wildlife habitats.

The animal kingdom is full of amazing creatures, from lions and tigers to whales and monkeys. We'll explore why it's important to protect these animals and their habitats, including the significance of animal symbolism in different cultures.

Lastly, we'll discover the beauty and importance of flowers. Not only are they beautiful, but they also play an important role in medicine, perfume, and other cultural customs. We'll also learn about gardening and the significance of preserving natural resources.

Through all of these wonders, we'll talk about the importance of taking care of our planet and helping preserve its beauty. Join us for a journey of discovery and understanding about the natural world around us.

CHAPTER 1

GOODNIGHT TO THE SUN

The sunset is a breathtaking natural event that has fascinated people since the beginning of time. The warm and vibrant colors of orange, pink, and red and the contrast of light and shadow create an awe-inspiring sight that has inspired poets, artists, and writers for centuries. The sun slowly sinking below the horizon signals the end of a day and the beginning of the night, bringing a sense of closure and a mixture of emotions of melancholy and beauty.

The sunset is more than just a physical phenomenon; it is also a cultural phenomenon. Different communities and civilizations around the world have created their unique ways of saying farewell to the sun, honoring it for its life-giving power and its role in shaping the world. Some cultures light candles, others sing songs, and some engage in elaborate ceremonies involving dance and prayer. These rituals reflect a deep reverence for nature and the cycle of life and death, birth, and ending.

In this chapter, we will explore the different customs and traditions of bidding farewell to the sun from various parts of the world. We will learn about the ancient Egyptians, who worshiped the sun god Ra, the Indigenous people of North America, who have rich cultural traditions of sun dance ceremonies, and the people of Japan, who practice various rituals and festivals to celebrate the setting sun. We will explore each culture's different insights and beliefs about the sun and the reasons for honoring it.

Furthermore, we will also examine the scientific aspects of the sunset, which is a spectacular display of the physics of light, color, and reflection. We will learn about the different phases that take place with the movements of the sun, such as the golden hour, the blue hour, and the green flash. We will also talk about the ways light travels through the atmosphere and how this creates the vibrant colors seen during sunsets.

Finally, we will consider the philosophical and spiritual significance of the sunset and our connection with the universe. The sunset is a reminder that everything in the world is interconnected, and the same sun that sets in one place is the same sun that rises in another. The sunset presents an opportunity for reflection and contemplation, as we recognize our place in the vastness of the universe.

In conclusion, the sunset is more than just a stunning visual display; it is a cultural, scientific, and philosophical phenomenon that has held great significance for people throughout the world. By exploring the sunset from various perspectives, we can gain a deeper appreciation of this natural wonder and reflect upon our connection to the world around us.

The sunset is a magical time of day that brings out some of the most beautiful colors in the sky. As the sun starts to go down, the sky transforms into a palette of colors that ranges from warm oranges, pinks, and reds to cool shades of purple and blue. The colors blend together in the sky, creating a breathtaking sight that is both peaceful and serene.

What makes each sunset so extraordinary is that no two sunsets are ever the same. The sky is always changing; the clouds move, and the colors shift as the sun goes down. It's like having a brand new painting to admire every single day.

Watching the sunset is a great way to relax and unwind after a long day. People love the sunset because of its calming effect on the mind and soul. It's so peaceful that some people even say that it helps them feel more relaxed and less stressed.

Many people have found creative ways to express their love for the evening sky. Some paint pictures, draw, or take photographs of the sunset, while others write poems or songs about it. These artistic expressions are a testament to the beauty of the sunset and the joy it brings to people's lives.

But, you don't need to be an artist to enjoy the sunset. All you need is a comfortable spot to sit and watch as the colors change in the sky. You might want to lean against a tree or sit on a bench to get a better view of the sky. Either way, taking in the sunset, even just for a few minutes, can be a great way to clear your mind and appreciate the simple beauty of the world around you.

In conclusion, the sunset is a part of nature that helps us appreciate the beauty of the world we live in. Each sunset is unique, and its colors and hues make for a breathtaking display that inspires us to think more deeply and feel more connected to the world. Whether you're an artist or just someone who enjoys the peacefulness of a beautiful sunset, it's something that everyone can appreciate. So, take a moment to sit back, relax, and enjoy the beauty of the sunset – you won't regret it!

As the sun begins to set each day, it creates breathtaking colors in the sky, inspiring different cultures throughout the world to honor this stunning moment in their unique and meaningful ways. These cultural rituals reflect a deep respect for nature and the significance of the sun's daily journey.

In ancient Egyptian mythology, the sun was an integral part of their belief system, representing the sun god Ra. Egyptians believed that the sun traveled through the heavens on a boat and returned to the underworld each night. To ensure a safe journey in the afterlife, they performed a ritual called "Opening the Mouth," where they recited sacred texts and performed elaborate ceremonies.

In other cultures, the sun is revered as a powerful force that provides life-giving energy. The sun dance is a significant Native American ritual practiced by various tribes in the United States and Canada. This ceremony involves a prolonged period of fasting, dance, and prayer, and the piercing of the skin with eagle talons to symbolize humility and offer thanks.

In Japan, the sunset is a moment of beauty and reflection. When the sun begins to set, locals practice "Yuuwakai," which involves gathering on a beach, watching the sunset, and writing "waka," a short form of Japanese poetry, to express their gratitude.

Other cultures celebrate the sunset through dance, music, or storytelling. In Bali, Indonesia, locals practice the Kecak dance, which involves chanting, hand-clapping, and the movement of over a hundred performers.

These cultural rituals highlight the beauty and significance of the sunset, reminding us of the importance of respecting nature and its beauty. They inspire us to connect with the natural world and appreciate its wonders, reflecting on our place in the universe. By paying tribute to the sun's journey each day, these diverse cultures show their appreciation for the natural world and remind us of the significance of the sunset in our shared human experience.

In this chapter, we have explored the sunset from different perspectives, including cultural, scientific, and philosophical viewpoints. We have seen how this natural phenomenon has inspired people throughout history, from ancient Egyptians, Native Americans, and Japanese to modern-day cultures around the world.

The sunset is a breathtaking event that showcases a spectacular display of light, color, and reflection. As the sun starts to go down, the sky transforms into a palette of warm oranges, pinks, and reds to cool shades of purple and blue. These colors blend together in the sky, creating a breathtaking sight that is both peaceful and serene. What makes each sunset so unique is that no two sunsets are ever the same. The sky is always changing, and the colors shift as the sun goes down, creating different hues and shades every day.

We have examined how cultural rituals reflect a deep respect for nature and the sun's daily journey. For ancient Egyptians, the sun represented the sun god Ra; they believed that the sun traveled through the heavens on a boat, and when it disappeared below the horizon, they performed a ritual called "Opening the Mouth" to ensure a safe journey in the afterlife. Native Americans practiced the sun dance, a significant ritual that involves fasting, dance, prayer, and piercing the skin, symbolizing humility and gratitude. In Japan, locals practice "Yuuwakai," a moment of beauty and reflection, gathering on a beach to watch the sunset and express their gratitude for nature's beauty.

Moreover, we have also examined the scientific aspects of the sunset. We have learned how light travels through the atmosphere, creating different phases of the sky, such as the golden hour, the blue hour, and the green flash. We have also seen how the behaviors of light and color create the beautiful shades and hues we see during sunsets, making each sunset a unique work of art.

The sunset reminds us that everything in the world is interconnected, and by embracing it, we gain a deeper appreciation of the natural world. Whether we're artists, poets, writers, or people who just love the peacefulness of a beautiful sunset, we can all appreciate its beauty. There's no need to rush through life; the sunset allows us to slow down, breathe, and reflect. It's a moment of tranquility and a chance to appreciate and celebrate the beauty of life around us.

In conclusion, the sunset is a profound and fascinating natural event that has long captivated people worldwide. The beauty, warmth, and colors of the sunset symbolize life, hope, and renewal.

■■

CHAPTER 2

GOODNIGHT TO THE STARS

As the sun sets and darkness descends upon the world, the stars emerge, twinkling and shimmering in the expanse of the nighttime sky. The vastness of space causes us to ponder, and the constellations provide a familiar map for our journey into the unknown. Throughout history, humans have looked up at the nighttime sky and found meaning in the stars. In this chapter, we will explore the constellations, their significance in different cultures, and how humanity has been captivated by the beauty of the nighttime sky.

The Greeks were known for their mythological stories of the stars that have been passed down through the ages. The twelve constellations in the Zodiac, including Aries, Taurus, and Gemini, were believed to represent mythological figures and animals. According to Greek mythology, the skies were divided into two parts, one ruled over by Zeus and the other by his brother Poseidon. The stars and constellations were believed to be the creations of the gods, who placed them in the sky as a symbol of their power.

The ancient Chinese also had their own beliefs about the stars. For them, the stars represented the 4 basic elements (water, fire, earth, and wood) and the cosmic balance of Yin and Yang. They also developed astrological practices that drew upon the positions of the stars in the sky to predict people's futures.

Beyond their cultural significance, the beauty of the nighttime sky and the wonder of stargazing have captured human imagination for centuries. Stargazing has been a source of inspiration for artists, writers, and astronomers alike. Writers like Jules Verne and H.G. Wells depicted otherworldly adventures amongst the stars, while music virtuoso Gustav Holst composed "The Planets" suite, which draws inspiration from the astrological characterizations of the planets.

Astronomers have continued to marvel at the nighttime sky, leading to numerous scientific discoveries. From Galileo's first use of a telescope to observe the moons of Jupiter to the recent images captured by the Hubble telescope, stargazing has fostered scientific exploration and enriched our understanding of the universe.

For centuries, humans have been fascinated by the stars in the nighttime sky. The beauty and majesty of the stars have captured human imagination, leading to a rich tradition of storytelling and culture building through the use of constellations. A constellation is a group of stars forming a recognizable pattern that has been associated with a particular figure, animal or object. Throughout history, different cultures have developed their own interpretations, stories, and significance behind these constellations.

The Greeks are an excellent example of a culture that used constellations to understand and relate to the world around them. They saw the stars as the gods looking down on them from above, and they created intricate stories of these gods and their lives in the sky, using them to explain natural phenomena and convey important morals. For example, it is said that the constellation Andromeda was created when a beautiful princess was punished by the gods for her mother's arrogance by being chained to a rock and left to be devoured by a sea monster. She was rescued by a hero named Perseus, who later married her and was placed among the stars.

In contrast, the ancient Chinese saw the sky as a manifestation of harmony and balance within the universe.

Chinese astronomy placed great importance on the movements of celestial bodies, reflecting the principles of Daoism and Confucianism. They created their own set of constellations, many of which are based on mythological stories and are associated with animals rather than gods. The most well-known constellation in Chinese astronomy is the Big Dipper. It is known as the "Northern Dipper," and the stars represent seven important gods of the Daoist religion.

The ancient Egyptians also had their own constellations, which were associated with their pantheon of gods and goddesses. Their interest in the sky was inextricably linked to their beliefs about death and life after death. The Duat, the realm of the gods and the dead, was believed to be a mirror of the nighttime sky, reflected in the patterns of the stars and constellations. One of the most famous constellations for the ancient Egyptians was Orion, which they viewed as the god Osiris, god of the afterlife.

Lastly, the Polynesian cultures and their many islands developed various constellations that drew upon their seafaring cultures. These cultures relied on the stars to navigate their journeys across the ocean, so constellations held a special significance for their way of life. The most well-known example is the Southern Cross, which aided Polynesian sailors in navigation across the southern seas.

In conclusion, constellations are a powerful tool for humanity, providing a means to explore and understand the vast expanse of the nighttime sky. Every culture has developed its constellations, and behind each of them, there is a unique story and a carefully woven history that reflects their beliefs and way of life. Whether used for sailing across oceans or understanding the divine, constellations always carry rich symbolism and significance - connecting us to the eternal mystery of the stars.

In conclusion, join us in this chapter as we navigate the different constellations that light up the nighttime sky and learn about their cultural and scientific significance. Let us explore the beauty of stargazing and discover the secrets and wonders of the cosmos. As we peer out into the depths of space, we are reminded that there is still so much to learn and discover, and that the nighttime sky continues to inspire us with its beauty and majesty.

The nighttime sky is a visual symphony of beauty, a kaleidoscope of twinkling stars and boundless space that has beckoned mankind since the dawn of time. It is a canvas upon which nature has painted its most exquisite masterpiece, and it never fails to elicit a sense of awe and amazement in those who marvel at its grandeur. As we gaze up at the stars, we are transported to another world, a world of infinite potential and possibility. We are greeted by a moment of pure tranquility that invites us to spend a moment in contemplation and reflection.

When we look up at the sky, we not only observe its beauty but also feel a sense of connection with something beyond ourselves. The stars have always had a mystical quality about them, evoking feelings of wonder, curiosity and even spirituality. It's almost as if they hold a secret, a hidden meaning that we strive to decipher. We are captivated by the way they sparkle and glimmer, each one a point of light in the vastness of space. It is these qualities that have inspired countless artists, poets and writers throughout history to try and capture the enchantment of the nighttime sky in their works.

However, the stars are not just an object of artistic interpretation, but they have also been studied scientifically to help us understand the mysteries of the universe. The study of the cosmos has been a source of fascination to scientists for centuries, and through technology such as telescopes and spacecraft, we have been able to gaze deeper into space and gain an understanding of the universe that was once unimaginable. With each new discovery, we marvel at the scale and complexity of the universe, and our appreciation of its beauty and wonder only deepens.

Despite our modern technological advances that allow us to study the stars in greater detail, the primitive urge to look up at the sky remains with us. It's a grounding experience that connects us to the universal consciousness and reminds us of the infinite possibilities that lie before us. Looking up at the stars is a moment of transience, as we are reminded that we are a tiny speck in the grand scheme of the universe, yet it's a moment that fills us with wonder and awe.

In conclusion, the nighttime sky is not simply a visual spectacle, but a gateway to the universe that inspires us to contemplate and explore the mysteries of the cosmos. Whether we gaze up alone or with others, the stars evoke feelings of unity and connection that unify us with the timeless and eternal beauty of nature. It's a moment of transformative beauty, a reminder that there is always beauty to be found in the natural wonders that surround us.

In conclusion, the nighttime sky has been a source of fascination for humanity since the beginning of time. The beauty of the stars and the vastness of space have captivated our attention, invoking feelings of wonder, awe, and contemplation. Throughout history and across cultures, the stars have played a significant role in inspiring myths, legends, and works of art, as well as scientific exploration and discovery. The constellations that light up the sky have provided a means for us to navigate the night, understand the world around us, and connect with something more profound than ourselves.

This chapter explored the significance of the constellations in different cultures, and how they have been used as a map of the night sky to understand the universe and our place in it. From the stories of Greek Mythology through to the Chinese Astrology, the constellations have been linked with deities, animals, and even cultural practices, providing insight into human culture and beliefs. The stars have captivated humanity's imagination, and this has led to innovative scientific discoveries, including mapping the universe with telescopes and space probes and the discovery of several planets orbiting distant stars.

Despite the incredible progression of science and technology, stargazing remains a grounding experience for humanity. Gazing up at the nighttime sky, we are reminded of both the vastness and transience of our existence. This feeling of humility connects us with the greater cosmos and cultivates a sense of wonder and appreciation for the universe's beauty and mystery. Stargazing continues to be an experience that connects us across time and culture. Sharing this moment with others allows us to understand the similarities and differences between our beliefs and cultural practices and creates a sense of community and unity.

In conclusion, the stars remind us of our place in the universe, and the constellations light up our journey. The nighttime sky continues to be a source of fascination, sparking cultural beliefs, artistic inspiration, scientific discovery, and personal reflection. The stars are a universal language that connects us with something beyond ourselves and unites humanity in our appreciation and contemplation of natural wonders that surround us.

CHAPTER 3

GOODNIGHT TO THE SEAS

Goodnight to the Seas takes us on a fascinating journey through the captivating world of the ocean and its creatures. With awe-inspiring wonders such as whales, dolphins, and seahorses, the ocean world presents a breathtaking view of nature's diversity. Yet, human activities, such as overfishing and pollution, have led to an unsettling decline of marine life, putting their existence under threat.

In this chapter, we'll explore the mesmerizing world of the ocean, and dive deep to discover the adaptations that sea creatures employ to thrive in their environment. We'll learn about dolphins that frolic around in the waves, whales that sing sweet melodies deep in the abyss, and seahorses that move gracefully through swaying beds of seaweed.

However, amidst all that wonder, we'll also confront some uncomfortable truths. Human impact on the ocean has endangered the ocean's biodiversity, which leads to a catastrophe for marine ecosystems. We'll discuss the importance of sea conservation and the need for humans to protect marine life. The ocean is home to creatures that hold the key to critical medical advancements, and their survival could be key in fighting life-threatening diseases.

Ultimately, this chapter is a call to action, a plea to humans to acknowledge our role in the deterioration of the ocean and take action to preserve these natural wonders before it's too late.

So, grab your mask and snorkel, and dive into Chapter, as we explore this beautiful world while learning what we can do to help conserve marine life.

Have you ever felt the call of the ocean? Beneath the waves lies a captivating world of wonder waiting to be discovered. From the tiniest plankton to the largest whales, the ocean is home to an incredible array of creatures. It's a world that's both majestic and mysterious, with each creature having its unique traits and features.

Sharks, for example, have a reputation as fierce predators, but they play a vital role in the ocean's ecosystem. They help regulate populations of other marine animals, allowing a healthy balance in the environment. Despite their fearsome appearance, sharks are also fascinating creatures with unique characteristics and behaviors.

Whales, on the other hand, are gentle giants, known for their impressive size and power. Watching a whale gracefully swim through the ocean is an experience that leaves you feeling humbled and awed. And let's not forget their beautiful songs, which are complex and hauntingly beautiful.

Dolphins are also a favorite of many ocean-lovers. Their playful and intelligent nature has captured the hearts of people for generations. They are social animals and love to communicate with each other in a unique language of chirps and whistles that are both fascinating and mesmerizing.

Sea turtles, with their ancient history and unique life cycle, are also a marvel of the ocean. Their journey from hatchling to maturity is full of challenges and obstacles, making their survival even more incredible.

Exploring the wonders of the ocean and its creatures is an adventure that is nothing short of thrilling. Each encounter with a sea creature is a humbling reminder of the world's vastness and natural beauty. So, why not grab your sunscreen, put on your snorkel gear, and dive into the ocean's mesmerizing world of wonders?

Whales:

Of all the creatures that inhabit the ocean, whales are some of the most magnificent. Their sheer size and beauty can leave us in awe while reminding us of how small we really are in the grand scheme of things. Despite their immensity, whales move through the water with an incredible grace that captures our imagination.

There are different types of whales - some are smaller, while others can grow up to 100 feet in length. The blue whale, in particular, is known for being the largest creature on earth, weighing in at a staggering 200 tons. Despite their size, they are peaceful creatures who exhibit complex emotions and intelligence.

Whales are also social creatures, and they often travel in large groups. Within their pods, they exhibit behaviors that show their intelligence and social bonds, such as parenting and mourning their dead. But perhaps the most memorable behavior of whales is when they leap out of the water and come crashing down with a splash, a move known as breaching. It's an awe-inspiring sight that never fails to thrill and excite.

Unfortunately, due to hunting, pollution, and other human activities, the population of some whale species has been threatened. That's why it's important that we all do our part to protect these gentle giants and their habitat, so that our children and future generations can also experience the wonder of whales in the wild.

If you ever get the chance to see a whale in the ocean, it's an experience that you will never forget-- the sound of their songs, the sight of them breaching, and the feel of their presence convey a sense of awe and beauty beyond words. Whales are a true reminder of the magnificence of nature, and we need to protect them for the sake of our planet as well as for the next generation.

Dolphins:

Dolphins are some of the most remarkable creatures in the ocean. They are intelligent, playful, and curious animals that have captured our imaginations for generations. Their natural grace and ability to swim make them a joy to watch in their natural habitat.

Dolphins are part of the cetacean family, which includes whales and porpoises. Like all cetaceans, dolphins have a streamlined body shape and long tails that make them excellent swimmers. They can reach speeds of up to 20 miles per hour and can swim massive distances. They also have a dynamic language of clicks, whistles, and physical movements to communicate with each other.

Dolphins are also very social animals that live together in groups, called pods. In these pods, dolphins communicate and exhibit behaviors that show their remarkable intelligence and emotional bonds. They care for each other's young, cooperate when finding food, and show a range of emotions, including joy, happiness, and excitement.

One of the most unique and beloved aspects of dolphins is their playful nature. They love to frolic and interact with each other and even with humans in the wild. They often ride the waves alongside boats, jump out of the water, and do flips in the air. Their love of play is one that has endeared them to people all over the world.

Unfortunately, dolphins are also threatened by human activities, including overfishing, pollution, and entanglement in fishing nets. Many dolphin populations worldwide have suffered due to these factors, making conservation efforts essential for their survival.

Swimming with dolphins is a dream come true for many people. It is an incredible experience to witness these creatures up close and in their natural habitat. However, we must also recognize that dolphins are wild animals, and as such, we must always act responsibly and ethically around them.

Overall, dolphins are remarkable creatures, and it is our job to protect them and their natural habitats. By educating ourselves and others about these amazing animals, we can take the first steps towards ensuring their continued existence and sharing the gifts of our planet with those who come after us.

Seahorses:

Seahorses are truly remarkable animals with unique characteristics that set them apart from other marine life. They belong to the family Syngnathidae, which includes pipefish and sea dragons, and are easily recognizable by their upright posture, elongated snouts, and delicate appearance. They can be found in shallow tropical and temperate waters all around the world, from Australia to the Caribbean.

One of the most striking features of seahorses is their upright posture and elongated snouts. They use these snouts for feeding, sucking in tiny crustaceans and plankton like a vacuum cleaner. Their prehensile tails are also essential components of their feeding behavior. Seahorses use their tails to anchor themselves in the water, so they can remain stationary while waiting for food to drift by.

Seahorses come in a variety of colors and patterns, with some species resembling leaves, twigs, or coral formations. This remarkable ability to blend in with their surroundings allows them to avoid predators and remain concealed from potential prey.

Male seahorses are unique in that they're the only animal species where males carry and care for their offspring. The female seahorse produces large eggs that they deposit into a specialized pouch located on the male's belly. The male then fertilizes the eggs and carries them for the duration of their gestation. The Dad seahorse "gives birth" by contracting his abdominal muscles to expel the babies out of his pouch, sending them into the ocean currents.

Despite being fascinating creatures, many species of seahorses are threatened due to habitat destruction, overfishing and the exotic pet trade. Some types of seahorses are also used in traditional Chinese medicine, which contributes to their decline.

Efforts have been initiated to conserve seahorse populations. Marine biologists recommend responsible fishing methods, creating marine protected areas, and monitoring of the illegal trade of these animals. With appropriate conservation measures, we can help to preserve the habitat of these fantastic creatures and keep their populations thriving.

In summary, Seahorses are unique examples of marine life distinguished by their upright posture, elongated snouts, and delicate bodies. Their feeding behaviors, vibrant coloring and distinctive appearance make them captivating examples of sea creatures. Their unusual reproductive strategy of fathers carrying and nurturing their offspring is awe-inspiring. In many areas, seahorse populations are in decline, and conservation measures have proven to be a vital step towards protecting these remarkable species. Seahorses are deserving of our admiration and need for preservation to keep them a part of our ocean ecosystem.

Sharks are one of the most diverse and unique species of fish on the planet. There are over 500 documented species of sharks that come in a wide range of colors, shapes, and sizes. Some, like the whale shark, are gentle giants that move slowly and filter feed, while others, such as the great white shark, are incredibly fast and powerful apex predators. Sharks are found in all of the world's oceans, from shallow reef systems to the deep, dark depths of the open sea.

One of the most well-known traits of sharks is their reputation as dangerous animals. While it's true that some species, such as the bull and tiger sharks, are responsible for attacks on humans, the vast majority of sharks pose little threat. In fact, almost all shark species are harmless to humans, and only a handful are known to be aggressive. Humans are not a part of their natural diet, and most attacks occur when sharks mistake humans for more typical prey or during incidents caused by humans provoking sharks. It also should be noted that humans pose a far greater threat to sharks than the other way around. Sharks have been overfished and hunted for years, particularly for their fins used to make shark fin soup and for their meat, causing many species to be listed as threatened or endangered.

Sharks are unique in that they have evolved to occupy many different ecological niches in the ocean. They are found at every level of the ocean's food chain, from the tiny pygmy shark that grows only to about 6 inches long and feeds on smaller fish and plankton to the gigantic whale shark that feeds primarily on plankton. Larger sharks such as the great white shark, tiger shark and hammerhead shark are apex predators, feeding on smaller fish, squid, and marine mammals. These sharks play a crucial role in regulating the populations of these animals and keeping the ocean's ecosystem in check.

One notable adaptation of sharks is their ability to detect prey using their incredible sense of smell. Sharks can detect the smallest traces of blood in the ocean, allowing them to locate prey even from miles away. They also have highly acute vision, which makes it easy for them to spot movement in the water and hunting prey.

Many sharks have a unique relationship with their environment, and some rely on specific habitats for survival. For instance, the grey reef shark is commonly found near coral reefs, while the angel shark is adapted for life on the ocean floor. Some species spend their entire lives in the same area, like the silvertip shark, never wandering far from their home base.

In sectors such as the Galapagos Islands, eco-tourism has helped give a new means of conservation. People can now go on boats and observe sharks in their natural habitats without doing any harm to the creatures. They can appreciate the animals' value through the careful introduction of guidelines to prevent causing sharks any harm.

In summary, sharks are unique animals that are essential to the ecological health of our oceans. Though some species are dangerous to humans, most sharks pose little threat, and overfishing poses a far greater threat to their survival. Their keen senses and remarkable adaptations make them fascinating creatures that occupy crucial roles in their habitats. Knowing and admiring these amazing animals are important in implementing conservation measures to help future shark populations and promote healthy oceans. By understanding the role of these incredible creatures, we can help ensure that the world's oceans remain healthy, balanced ecosystems, and that these magnificent animals continue to thrive.

The oceans are a critical part of our ecosystem, and they play a crucial role in regulating the Earth's climate and supporting the biosphere's balance. The ocean environments are home to numerous marine creatures and plant life, each with its unique function and role to play in maintaining the earth's development. However, human activities over the past few decades have significantly impacted marine ecosystems, leading to a sharp decrease in biodiversity and an increase in environmental damage. This growing evidence demands the need for more effective sea conservation efforts to reduce further damage, protect marine life, and ensure a sustainable future for our planet.

Overfishing is among the leading threats to marine life, especially those exploited by commercial fisheries.

Industrial fishing techniques, such as bottom trawling, have hammered the sea floors, destroying coastal habitats and reducing the ocean depths biodiversity. The lack of regulations on target catch, poor management, and an ever-increasing global population who rely on seafood for survival exacerbate this problem.

Pollution is another significant concern in the oceanic environment. Plastic waste has accumulated extensively in the ocean's surface waters, adversely affecting sea animals by causing injuries, entanglement, and death. Polluted waters are also detrimental to marine plants such as seaweed, which forms the foundation on which countless marine creatures depend upon for shelter and food. Ocean pollution goes beyond plastics and includes oil spills, chemical pollutants, and toxic waste, which cause long-term environmental damage.

The impacts of climate change are already apparent in the ocean environment, which influences sea temperature, ocean acidification, habitat degradation, and the shifting of marine species' geographical location. As ocean temperatures continue to change, coral reefs are progressively bleaching, and many other marine species are experiencing significant changes in their lifecycle and migratory patterns, directly affecting the ocean's food chain.

Marine conservation measures are essential to promote ocean health, protect marine life and preserve biodiversity. Governments and stakeholders around the world must actively work together to develop effective policies and solutions to reduce harmful effects and invest in protecting vulnerable ecosystems. This could include sustainable fishing practices, policies on coastal management, limiting carbon emissions, and banning pollutants that can significantly pollute marine environments.

Additionally, individuals must contribute by adopting eco-friendly habits and proper waste management. Reducing the usage of single-use plastics, recycling, and efficiently disposing of waste can significantly contribute to ocean conservation. People can also have an impact on responding to local conservation schemes through donations or volunteer programs.

In conclusion, the oceans are vital to our planet's ecological balance and our very existence as humans. The situation calls for critical action to guarantee that marine life thrives and the ocean remains healthy. Conjointly, everyone can work together for the conservation of global marine reserves by raising awareness or adopting eco-friendly habits. With proper collaboration and engagement, we can make a significant positive impact on such pressing issues. Starting with simple things can lead to a larger scale of difference-making, leading to restoring the vitality in our oceans and the protection of marine life.

In conclusion, "Goodnight to the Seas" reminds us of the breathtaking diversity and complexity of the ocean's ecosystems and the importance of protecting them. The chapter serves as a warning that without appropriate action, these awe-inspiring environments could be lost forever. The degradation of the world's water bodies as a result of human action is a significant concern, necessitating a change in our way of life. This involves altering the ways in which we consume and dispose of products, as well as developing new policies to address the current status quo of our oceans.

Furthermore, the chapter encourages us to apply our collective knowledge of ocean conservation to establish and implement effective solutions. These solutions include promoting sustainable fishing practices, limiting plastic waste, and reducing our carbon footprint. The magnitude of the problem necessitates international cooperation to enact solutions. Governments need to intensify their efforts in ocean conservation and incentivize the private sector. Simultaneously, non-profit organizations and individuals must work together to advocate for change.

Finally, "Goodnight to the Seas" provides hope and a blueprint for the future. Through collective actions and changes in human behavior, we can preserve the ocean's ecosystems, ensuring that the oceans remain healthy and vibrant for generations to come. We must recognize our responsibility to act now and take care of our planet's future, protecting our oceans, and maintaining its wonders. The oceans remind us of our interconnectedness, and preserving them is necessary for the future of our planet and the human race.

■■

CHAPTER 4

GOODNIGHT TO THE FORESTS

Forests are some of the most breathtaking and crucial features of our planet. They give us oxygen, purify the air we breathe, and absorb one of the main greenhouse gases that cause climate change. Homes for millions of plant and animal species, forests provide us with a diverse ecosystem that keeps our world in balance. From enormous trees and thriving undergrowth to predatory carnivores and elusive herbivores, forests are a complex and fascinating world.

Despite everything forests do for us, they're under threat. Humans have been tearing down forests at an alarming rate for farming and land development purposes, leading to a sharp decline in their numbers worldwide. Unfortunately, the loss of forests worldwide has led to a loss of habitats for animals and plants and negatively impacted the ecosystem on a global scale. For example, the Amazon rainforest is often called the lungs of the earth, and its destruction could create serious environmental problems globally.

It's essential to understand the gravity of the situation and work towards effective solutions. We must protect the forests and the animals who rely on them for survival, as well as the many services these habitats provide for us humans. The essay will explore the beauty and significance of the world's forests and highlight the impact deforestation has had on wildlife habitats. It will also discuss the importance of reforestation as an essential step in protecting wildlife habitats and preserving our environment for future generations.

Forests are among the most vibrant and complex environments on earth, home to millions of species of plants and animals. A single forest can contain more plant and animal species than many countries, making forests a priceless asset to the world. They are critical for the health of our planet and provide numerous benefits to humans, from purifying the air we breathe to protecting the soil from erosion. Forests are also essential for human well-being and can provide us with clean water, food, and medicine.

The beauty of forests lies in their diversity. From towering trees to the smallest of shrubs, the landscape in forests is ever-changing and always stunning. Forests are home to a vast variety of animal species, from the majestic Bengal

Tiger to the nimble monkeys. These animals are known to contribute to forest regeneration, and their activities, such as pollination and seed dispersion, also benefit other plant species. The hues of the forest are always a sight to behold. The way sunlight breaks through the canopy, illuminating the intricate shadows and beautiful foliage.

Forests play a crucial role in mitigating climate change. Trees absorb carbon dioxide from the atmosphere and store it, making forests an enormous carbon sink. In this way, forests help to reduce the negative impacts of human activities on the environment, helping to stabilize the earth's climate. Deforestation, on the other hand, is one of the primary contributors to climate change, with lost carbon sinks that lead to more carbon dioxide in the air. Trees also help regulate the water cycle, preventing soil erosion and protecting against floods and droughts.

Forests play an essential role in the lives of millions of people worldwide. They are sources of food, income, recreation, and even spiritual and cultural significance. Local communities often have a deep connection with the forests, knowing the importance of the ecosystem to their physical and economic survival. Some people gain employment and income by working in the forest conservation industry, such as forest management, the timber industry, and ecotourism.

Forests also offer recreational activities such as camping, hiking, and fishing.

In addition to the environmental benefits, forests are also essential for the economic and social development of communities around the world. Many people rely on forests for their livelihoods, including the logging and timber industries, ecotourism, and traditional forms of agriculture. Forests are also home to a vast variety of indigenous people, who have sustained themselves and their communities for generations by living off the land. These communities are the guardians of their forests, and their traditional knowledge is valuable in the conservation of these ecosystems.

In conclusion, forests are a source of beauty and wonder, as well as essential to the survival of our planet. They provide a vast array of ecosystem services, from regulating the climate and water supply to providing us with vital resources such as food and medicine. It is our responsibility to protect and conserve these forests. We must work towards sustainable forest management practices and invest in reforestation efforts to restore damaged forest ecosystems. With concerted effort, we can ensure that the world's forests remain a beautiful, vital feature of our planet for generations to come.

Forests serve as home to millions of plant and animal species, making them one of the wealthiest ecosystems on earth. From towering trees to the smallest of insects, each organism plays an essential role in maintaining the complex balance of the forest ecosystem. Forests provide habitat, food, shelter, and breeding sites for diverse animal species.

Mammals are among the most widely recognized forest inhabitants, with some species, such as the Bengal tiger, giant pandas, jaguars, and black bears, catching the eye for their beauty and power. Many other mammals, such as deer, squirrels, raccoons, and opossums, play vital roles in the forest. For example, deer help to propagate certain plant species by dispersing seeds.

Birds are also among the animal species that call the forest their home. Forests provide nesting, feeding, and breeding habitat for a wide range of bird species, including woodpeckers, owls, hawks, and eagles. These birds help to pollinate plants and regulate insect populations, such as the woodpecker that controls insect populations by feeding on them.

Reptiles and amphibians are equally important in the forest ecosystem. Frogs, toads, salamanders, turtles, and snakes are commonly found in the forest and play critical roles in nutrient cycling, pest control, and pollination. For example, the northern red salamander is an important predator of insect and invertebrate species and serves as a prey item for larger predators like birds and mammals.

Among the insects in the forest are pollinators, like bees and butterflies, which play an important role in plant reproduction. There are also many insect species that are decomposers, breaking down dead plant matter and organic materials to release essential nutrients back into the soil, helping new plants to thrive.

In conclusion, forests represent an essential habitat for many plant and animal species, which altogether create and support a complex and unique ecosystem. Their interwoven relationships help support the environment. All of the species play a crucial role in the forest, with each organism doing their part to maintain the delicate balance of the ecosystem. As such, we must protect and conserve our precious forests, so that the animal kingdom thrives and continues benefitting our environment.

Mammals:

Forests are among the most diverse ecosystems on the planet, teeming with life of all kinds, including some of the most iconic mammals in the world. Mammals such as tigers, jaguars, bears, elephants, and gorillas, call the forest their natural habitat. Forests are home to a wide variety of mammal species that are essential to the forest ecosystem, including deer, squirrels, raccoons, possums, and monkeys, among others.

Tigers are one of the most recognizable and beloved mammals found in the forest. These majestic creatures once roamed the forests of Asia, but today their population numbers have dwindled significantly due to habitat destruction and hunting. Forests provide tigers with essential cover and prey, allowing them to live, grow, and reproduce, making them an integral part of the forest's ecosystem.

Jaguars are another big cat species found in the forest. They're also one of the largest predators in the Amazonian rainforest, known for their hunting skills and powerful jaws. Jaguars play a critical role in keeping the forest ecosystem stable and healthy by controlling the population of herbivores.

Elephants are slow-moving giants that have a crucial place in the forest ecosystem. They play an important role in shaping the forest and maintaining its ecological balance. Elephants eat and disperse thousands of seeds every day, helping to create openings for new growth. By disturbing the soil and removing dead trees, elephants also help in the forest's nutrient cycle.

Gorillas, the largest primates in the world, dwell in the humid forests of central Africa. They're herbivores, feeding on a wide range of leaves and fruits, as well as the occasional small animal. Gorillas are essential dispersers of seeds, which helps maintain the ecological balance of the forest.

Bears are another group of mammals that inhabit forests like the grizzly, black, and polar bears. Their thick fur helps them to stay warm during colder months. These animals play an essential role in controlling the populations of herbivores in the forest, and they contribute significantly to the process of seed dispersal.

Other mammals such as deer, monkeys, raccoons, squirrels, and possums are also commonly found in the forest. These animals play a unique and vital role in the overall ecosystem of the forest. They all contribute to the ecological balance of the forest by controlling the populations of pests, pollinating flowers, helping to disperse seeds, and contributing nutrients to the soil, among other things.

In conclusion, forests are essential for the survival of many mammal species. These animals rely on the forest's resources for their shelter, food, and protection, making the forest ecosystem an essential part of their lives. As humans continue to encroach on the forest habitat for urbanization and industrialization, it is increasingly important to protect and preserve these ecosystems. By doing so, we can help ensure that these remarkable animals continue to thrive for generations to come!

Birds:

Forests aren't just home to incredible mammals - they're also home to a vast array of fascinating birds! From the distinctive calls of cuckoos to the hooting of owls and the soaring of eagles, the forest is alive with the sounds of birds. Many bird species require specific habitats, such as tree cavities, to nest in the forest, making it an essential part of their lives.

Cuckoos are one of the most common birds you'll hear in the forest. Their iconic call echoes through the trees and adds to the forest's natural soundscape. They're known for their brood parasitism behavior, which means they lay their eggs in other birds' nests and sometimes abandon their young. This behavior ensures the survival of their species as well as the birds that care for them.

Owls are another bird species that call the forest their home. They are skillful hunters due to their keen vision and hearing, and are known for their hooting sounds that cut through the forest's silence. Owls often make their homes in tree cavities that provide them with a natural habitat and refuge from predators.

Eagles are also common in the forest and are recognizable by their stunning wingspan and sharp talons. These birds of prey play a crucial role in controlling the populations of small rodents and fish, helping to maintain the balance of the forest ecosystem. Eagles often build their nests high up in trees to keep a watchful eye on their prey and protect their young.

Parrots are another bird species found in the forest. These colorful birds are known for their bright plumage and ability to mimic human speech. They often require specific habitats like tree cavities to nest. These birds play an important role in seed dispersal and are essential to the overall health of the forest ecosystem.

In conclusion, forests are home to a wide variety of bird species, each with its unique characteristics and behaviors. Birds are essential to the health and balance of the forest, providing necessary pollination and seed dispersal services. The forest also provides critical habitats for these birds, including tree cavities, which are crucial for their survival. By protecting the forests and the birds within them, we can ensure that these fascinating animals continue to thrive for many years to come.

Reptiles:

Forests are thriving ecosystems that support a wide variety of wildlife, including reptiles like snakes, lizards, and turtles. These fascinating creatures play an essential role in the forest's ecosystem by helping to regulate pest populations, adding to the diversity of the ecosystem, and maintaining the delicate balance that ultimately supports all life within it.

Snakes are one of the most well-known reptiles found in the forest, with various species adapted to different environments. They range from the arid deserts to the humid rainforests, relying heavily on their sense of smell, sight, and vibrations. Snakes are efficient hunters, using their keen senses and stealthy bodies to stalk their prey through the forest. Furthermore, they play an important role in controlling the populations of vertebrate and invertebrate pests, and even act as prey for numerous birds and mammals.

Lizards are another common type of reptile that thrives in forests. These creatures are well-adapted to live in rock crevices, the forest floor, or trees. They are also known for their incredible agility and ability to recover if they fall, making them one of the most resilient creatures in the forest. Lizards play an essential role in the forest's food web, eating insects, small animals, and plants. Some types of lizards, such as chameleons and gecko, are also renowned for their ability to change their color, making them difficult for predators to spot.

Turtles, with their slow-moving bodies, have adapted to living in wet environments, such as ponds, streams, and marshes. These creatures are known for their longevity and play an essential role in seed dispersal, pollination, and maintaining the balance of the wetland ecosystem. Turtles eat algae, aquatic plants, and small animals, and in turn, become food for larger predators, including otters and alligators.

In conclusion, reptiles are critical components of the forest ecosystem. They perform essential roles in regulating pest populations, pollination, seed dispersal, and also contribute to the forest's biodiversity. Protecting their delicate ecosystems is crucial to their survival, as well as for maintaining a sustainable and healthy forest. It is up to us to maintain the forests and reduce the damage caused by human activities so that we can ensure the protection and survival of these incredible reptiles for generations to come.

Amphibians:

Amphibians are fascinating creatures that live a dual life on land and in water. Frogs, toads, and salamanders are some of the most common species that live in forests. Forests provide a range of vital breeding habitats for many amphibians, with decaying tree trunks and leaf litter being some of the most important ones.

Forests are essential habitats for amphibians because they have damp areas that are crucial for laying eggs and sheltering young from predators and extreme weather. Amphibians lay their jelly-covered eggs in the water or on wet surfaces. The eggs absorb moisture from the environment, and then the emerging tadpoles or larvae feed on tiny organisms and develop in the water. The damp environment provides a safe haven that allows the young to grow without the risk of dehydration.

Decayed tree trunks and scattered leaves are also ideal habitats for amphibians. The decomposing wood creates an environment that is nutrient-rich and provides an abundance of food for the larvae. The leaves act as sponges that retain moisture, which reduces the risk of dehydration. Furthermore, the moist and cool environment provides a hiding place for the young from predators like snakes, birds, and small mammals.

Another reason why forests are crucial for amphibians is the abundance of insects and other small prey that live in them. Many amphibians, including frogs and toads, feed on insects and other small creatures that inhabit the forest floor. Salamanders, for instance, prey on small vertebrates such as worms, snails, and even small mammals.

However, amphibians are threatened globally because of habitat loss, pollution, disease, and climate change. Deforestation can cause environmental changes like soil erosion, changes in temperature, and water cycle regulation, which can significantly impact the survival of amphibians. The loss of habitats and the decline in environmental quality can reduce the availability of prey and breeding habitat, which can lead to population decline.

Therefore, it is essential to preserve forests and the habitats they provide for all species of animals, including amphibians. Forest conservation can help maintain healthy ecosystems, preserve prey availability, and protect breeding habitats, ensuring the survival of some of the world's most unique and important creatures.

Fish:

Forested streams and rivers are home to a rich diversity of fish species, including trout, salmon, and other cold-water fish. These fish require clean, cold water with a steady flow, which is often found in forested areas.

Forested streams and rivers offer a unique environment for these fish species. The forest canopy provides shade, which helps maintain cool water temperatures throughout the year. Trees and other vegetation that grow along the banks of streams help to filter and clean the water. This helps to ensure that the water is oxygen-rich and free of debris and pollutants.

Cold-water fish species are particularly vulnerable to changes in water temperature and water quality. Even small changes in water temperature or water quality can greatly affect their survival and reproductive success. Forested areas provide ideal conditions for these fish to thrive and reproduce.

Fish that live in forested streams and rivers play an essential role in freshwater ecosystems. They help regulate populations of insects, algae, and other aquatic organisms. This helps to maintain a healthy balance between different species, which is essential for the overall health of the ecosystem.

Despite the importance of forested streams and rivers for fish species, these habitats are under threat from a variety of human activities. One of the biggest threats to these habitats is deforestation. Clear-cutting of forests can lead to riverbank erosion, increased sedimentation, and reduced water quality. This can have a significant impact on fish populations, making it difficult for them to survive and reproduce.

Human activities such as mining, agriculture, and industry can also pollute waterways and reduce water quality. This can harm fish populations and their habitat. Climate change is also a significant threat, as it can cause changes in water temperature, precipitation patterns, and water availability.

As a result, fish populations may have to migrate to find suitable habitat.

To protect fish populations and their habitats, it is essential to preserve and conserve forested areas. Sustainable land-use practices and restoration projects can be implemented to help ensure the availability of clean, cold water for fish species. Watershed management plans can also help to maintain water quality and flow.

In addition, education and awareness programs can help to inform the public about the importance of preserving these habitats. This can help to foster a sense of stewardship and responsibility for the environment, which can ultimately benefit fish populations and other wildlife.

By taking steps to protect these unique environments, we can help ensure that forested streams and rivers continue to provide suitable habitat for cold-water fish species. These efforts will not only preserve the majestic beauty of these ecosystems, but they will also help to maintain healthy ecological systems for future generations.

Insects:

Forests are highly complex ecosystems that support a rich diversity of insect life. You can find millions of different species of insects living among the trees and undergrowth, from ants and beetles to butterflies and bees.

Insects play a critical role in forest ecosystems by contributing to a wide range of ecological processes. For example, many insects are pollinators that help plants reproduce. Bees, butterflies, and other pollinators transfer pollen from the male to the female parts of plants, allowing them to produce seeds and fruits. These seeds and fruits are consumed by many animals and make up the base of the food chain.

Insects also help control other insect populations by acting as predators or parasites. Ladybugs, for example, eat aphids and can help protect plants from damage. Some species of wasps are parasitic and lay their eggs inside the larvae or eggs of other insects, killing them and preventing them from developing.

Insects are also essential for the decomposition of dead plant and animal matter. Insects like beetles and flies feed on decaying matter and break it down into smaller pieces, which in turn are eaten by other decomposers, like fungi and worms. This decomposition process returns important nutrients to the soil, which help new plants grow.

Forested areas are under threat from a wide range of human activities including deforestation, conversion of natural habitats for agriculture and urbanization, and the overuse of pesticides. These activities can significantly negatively affect the diverse rich insect populations living in forests. Deforestation, for instance, destroys the habitat of forest insects, making it harder for them to survive. The overuse of pesticides can also harm beneficial insects like bees, butterflies, and ladybugs, as well as the insects they prey upon.

Protecting and preserving forested areas is essential in ensuring the health and survival of insect populations. We can help by promoting sustainable land-use practices and preserving forested habitats. Restoration projects, such as planting native vegetation, can also help to support insect populations.

Educating the public can also be an essential first step in insect conservation. Encouraging people to take action will spread awareness and promote ethical practices when using insecticides, especially by using methods and products that are less harmful to natural predators and beneficial insects.

Insects in the forest are all different, but they share the common goal of contributing to the health and balance of ecosystems. By conserving forests and promoting biodiversity, we can help ensure that insect populations thrive and continue to provide valuable ecological services. Ultimately, the healthy well-being of our forests is tied to the health of our planet, and that's why the conservation of insects in the forest is critical for sustaining life.

In conclusion, forests harbor a wide range of animal species, making them critical habitats for biodiversity conservation. The different species that live in the forest have adapted to its conditions, making them unique and fascinating to study. Protecting and conserving our forests is essential to ensure that these animals and their habitat continue to thrive for generations to come.

Deforestation, the cutting down of forests or removal of trees from a particular area, is a problem that has a far-reaching impact on the environment, economy, and society. One of the most critical and devastating consequences of deforestation is the loss and destruction of wildlife habitats. With the increasing habitat loss, many animal species are nearing extinction.

Wildlife and forests go hand in hand, and wildlife habitats are essential for animals' survival. Forests provide animals with a home, a sanctuary, a source of food, breeding grounds, and protection from predators. When we cut down forests, animals lose their homes and their source of food, forcing them to migrate to other areas in search of new habitats. For some species, this means they face endangerment, while others may face extinction. For example, rapid deforestation in the Amazon rainforest has resulted in the loss of habitats for animals like jaguars, tapirs, and monkeys, which could lead to their extinction.

One of the most effective ways to address habitat loss for wildlife is through reforestation, which involves planting new trees in areas where they were previously removed or destroyed. Reforestation provides a solution to the problem of deforestation and can help wildlife habitats recover. By planting trees, we can significantly impact the ecosystem and bring back the lost habitats for animals.

Reforestation has many benefits, such as creating new habitats for animals, reducing the effects of climate change, and fostering biodiversity. Trees help to trap carbon, absorb pollutants, reduce soil erosion, and stabilize the soil's water cycle. Forests are one of the most powerful natural solutions to climate change, providing the planet with an essential tool to mitigate the negative impacts of global warming.

However, there are factors that can hinder reforestation. One of the most notable ones is human activities such as logging, ranching, and farming, which have been the primary drivers of rainforest clearing. We cannot ignore the demand for commodities like beef, soy, and palm oil from these cleared lands. Timber logging, mining, industrial agriculture, and urbanization through human settlements are other leading causes of deforestation globally.

In conclusion, reforestation is a crucial component in the conservation of wildlife habitats, and we need to take a comprehensive approach to address deforestation. It's the responsibility of every one of us to do our part, whether it's through volunteering, donating, or raising awareness of the benefits of reforestation and tackling the root causes of deforestation. With the help of committed individuals, organizations, and governments worldwide, we can work towards effective solutions for habitat loss and protect wildlife species for generations to come.

Deforestation is a major issue that affects wildlife habitats and the planet as a whole. It involves cutting down trees and forests, usually to create space for farming, urbanization, or other human activities. Sadly, this has led to the degradation and destruction of wildlife habitats, which has negative impacts on animals and the environment.

Forests are home to millions of animal species, many of which are endangered or threatened. These animals depend on forests for shelter, food, and water, and when their habitats are cut down, they're left without a home. The loss of habitat puts additional pressure on these animals and can lead to population declines or extinction.

Deforestation also has other negative effects on the environment. Trees absorb carbon dioxide from the atmosphere and produce oxygen, which helps to maintain healthy air quality. When trees are cut down, there's less oxygen produced, and the amount of carbon dioxide released into the atmosphere increases. This can contribute to climate change, which has far-reaching implications for the planet.

The good news is that reforestation can help address some of these problems. Reforestation involves planting trees and restoring lost forests. It can help create new habitats for animals, improve air quality, conserve soil moisture, and reduce the impacts of climate change.

One important benefit of reforestation is that it helps reduce carbon dioxide levels in the atmosphere. Trees absorb carbon emissions from the environment, which helps to mitigate the effects of climate change. In fact, trees are considered one of the most effective ways to combat climate change.

Conservation efforts and reforestation projects can also protect and enhance biodiversity. By preventing deforestation, we can safeguard animal habitats and help maintain healthy ecosystems. Sustainable forest management practices can help ensure that forests are protected and managed in a way that benefits both animals and people.

In conclusion, deforestation has significant negative impacts on animal habitats and the environment. Reforestation and conservation efforts offer potential solutions to these problems. By planting new trees, protecting forests, and promoting sustainable forest management practices, we can protect wildlife habitats, improve the environment, and reduce the impacts of climate change.

CHAPTER 5

GOODNIGHT TO THE ANIMALS

Animals are fascinating creatures that come in all shapes and sizes, and they play an essential role in our environment. Sadly, many animal species around the world are in danger of extinction. The importance of conservation efforts cannot be underestimated as it plays a significant role in preserving the diversity of the animal kingdom for future generations to appreciate.

People all over the world have a rich history of using animals as symbols to represent different qualities. From the Eastern zodiac to many Indigenous cultures' totem poles, animals represent unique attributes and values. For instance, the elephant is a symbol of wisdom and strength, while the butterfly is a symbol of transformation and beauty. The use of animal symbolism helps us better understand and appreciate these creatures, as well as their role in our world.

Understanding the significance of animals in different cultures can also raise awareness of the importance of animal conservation. As we learn more about the important role that animals play, we become more aware of the threats they face. The pressures of habitat destruction, poaching, and climate change are only a few of the many factors that contribute to the decline of animal populations. With this knowledge, we are better equipped to support efforts aimed at protecting endangered species and promoting sustainable practices.

Conservation efforts take many forms, from saving habitats to preventing the spread of disease. These efforts require the involvement of many stakeholders, including governments, private organizations, and individuals. By supporting these efforts, we can help ensure that animals have a place to thrive and call home.

In conclusion, the animal kingdom is a vast and diverse world, worthy of our admiration and respect. From animal symbolism to conservation efforts, there's much to learn about these incredible creatures. By understanding the importance of animal conservation, we can work towards protecting endangered species and preserving their natural habitats. The message is clear: it's our duty to take care of these beautiful, majestic, and often vulnerable creatures.

The animal kingdom is a diverse and fascinating world, full of mystery and wonder. There are millions of different species that inhabit our planet, each with its unique characteristics and adaptations. Exploring the diversity of the animal kingdom is an exciting and enriching experience that can teach us so much about the natural world.

One of the most interesting things about animals is how they have evolved to survive in their respective environments. Adaptations can take many forms, from physical features like fins or wings, to more subtle changes like improved night vision or the ability to camouflage. Some animals even have specialized organs that allow them to sense the world in different ways, like the echolocation abilities of bats and dolphins.

Animals also come from an incredible variety of ecosystems. From the windswept tundras of the Arctic to the dense jungles of the Amazon, there's an enormous range of habitats where animals live. Many animals have adapted to these environments in unique ways, such as polar bears with their thick fur and insulated blubber or the sloth's ability to stay hidden high up in the trees.

Beyond the fascinating adaptations and unique environments, animals can also be incredibly beautiful. From bright and colorful birds to the patterns and markings on the skin of reptiles, each animal's look is unique and can be quite striking. When animals gather in large numbers, their movements and sounds can create spectacle and awe-inspiring moments, such as the annual migration of wildebeest in Africa or the synchronized displays of fireflies in Asia.

Exploring the diversity of the animal kingdom can also highlight the importance of conservation efforts. Many animals are threatened by habitat loss, climate change, poaching, and other human activities, and it's crucial to protect their habitats and promote sustainable practices to ensure the survival of these creatures.

In conclusion, exploring the diversity of the animal kingdom is a fascinating and vital pursuit that can teach us more about our world. Each animal has its unique role to play, and the complex webs of interaction between different species create intricate ecosystems that we are only beginning to understand. It's our responsibility to protect the natural world and its diverse inhabitants to ensure that future generations can continue to explore and appreciate the incredible beauty of the animal kingdom.

Endangered species are animals and plants that are at risk of becoming extinct. They face a wide range of threats, including habitat loss, climate change, pollution, hunting, and poaching. As humans, we have a responsibility to protect these creatures and their habitats, and conservation is key to achieving this.

So, why is conservation so important? For starters, endangered species play an integral role in keeping ecosystems healthy and balanced. Each species contributes to the delicate web of life, and the loss of even one species can cause a domino effect across the entire ecosystem. For example, bees and other pollinators are responsible for pollinating one-third of the world's crops, and without them, our food supply and economy would suffer tremendously.

In addition to their ecological importance, endangered species also have cultural and aesthetic values. Many species have deep cultural significance for indigenous communities around the world, and their loss can mean the erosion of cultural traditions and knowledge. Moreover, many endangered species are simply beautiful and awe-inspiring, and their loss would deprive us of the opportunity to marvel at the wonder and diversity of life on Earth.

To protect endangered species, a multifaceted approach is necessary. Habitat restoration is a critical component, as species need healthy and intact habitats to survive. Protecting animals from poaching and illegal trade is also essential. Many endangered species, such as elephants, rhinos, and tigers, are targeted by poachers for their valuable parts, such as ivory, horns, and bones.

Conservation efforts also rely heavily on education and awareness-raising. The more people understand the importance of protecting endangered species and their habitats, the more likely they are to take action. Non-governmental organizations (NGOs) and individuals can play an important role in supporting conservation efforts, whether by supporting research or raising awareness through social media and other means.

Finally, government policies and regulations play a huge role in protecting endangered species. Laws that safeguard habitats, limit hunting and poaching, and regulate the trade of endangered species can be critical in preventing their extinction. The Convention on International Trade in Endangered Species of Wild Fauna and Flora (CITES) is one such agreement that plays a vital role in regulating trade and helping to protect many endangered species.

In conclusion, conservation is essential for protecting endangered species and their habitats. It is necessary for the survival of the natural world, cultural heritage, and our well-being. Every one of us has a role to play in preserving our planet's biodiversity, and it's important that we work together to protect and conserve our natural world.

African elephants:

African elephants are one of the most fascinating animals on our planet, but sadly they're in danger of disappearing forever. There are many reasons why elephants are endangered, with poaching being one of the main causes. For years, people have hunted elephants for their ivory tusks, which are sold illegally on the black market. This has led to a sharp decline in elephant populations, with some herds losing up to 90% of their members.

Habitat loss is another major threat to African elephants. As human populations expand and grow, we take up more and more of their living space. This can mean that elephants don't have enough room to roam, food to eat, or water to drink. When they don't find what they need in the wild, they may turn to farms and villages in search of food, which can lead to conflicts with people.

Climate change is also a major factor affecting African elephants. The effects of global warming, things like droughts, floods, and wildfires, can make it even more difficult for these animals to find food and water. It can also lead to habitat loss and fragmentation, making it harder for elephants to migrate between different areas.

All of these challenges are contributing to a decline in the African elephant population. This is a huge concern for many reasons - elephants are a keystone species, meaning that they play a vital role in their ecosystem. They help shape the landscape by eating certain plants and supporting others, and they help maintain ecological balance by spreading seeds and keeping other species in check.

Thankfully, there are many people and organizations dedicated to protecting African elephants from these threats. One of the most important methods for protecting elephants is through anti-poaching patrols. These groups work to deter would-be poachers and stop them from killing elephants for their ivory. Others work on wildlife habitat conservation, restoration, and connectivity to create more room for elephants to roam and find food.

Public education and awareness-raising campaigns can also play a vital role in protecting elephants by teaching people how to live safely with these animals. Many organizations also run programs focused on reducing human-elephant conflicts and studying the elephants' behavior, so that scientists can better understand how to protect them.

In conclusion, African elephants are facing many challenges that are putting their future in jeopardy. Poaching, habitat loss, and climate change are among the most pressing issues, but by working together, we can help protect these amazing animals. It's up to all of us to support efforts to protect and preserve endangered species, including African elephants, and to take steps to live in harmony with the natural world.

Amur leopards:

Amur leopards are among the rarest big cats in the world, with only around 100 remaining in the wild. Sadly, these magnificent creatures are in danger of disappearing from the planet forever. There are several reasons why Amur leopards are endangered.

Habitat loss is one of the major threats facing the Amur leopard. As human populations grow, we're encroaching on more and more of their natural habitats. Logging, mining, and other industrial activities have destroyed large portions of the forests where these leopards live, leaving them with less and less space to hunt and roam. This can also lead to conflicts between leopards and humans, as they're forced to share a dwindling space.

Poaching is another major threat to Amur leopards. These animals are hunted for their fur and other body parts, which are sold illegally. Poachers target Amur leopards because of their rarity and the high demand for their fur in some countries. This makes them even more vulnerable to extinction.

Climate change is also affecting Amur leopards. As temperatures rise, their habitats are being altered, affecting their hunting and living patterns. Climate change can also reduce their prey base, making it harder for them to find food.

The decline in the Amur leopard population is a serious concern, not just because of the intrinsic value of these animals to the planet's biodiversity, but also because of their contribution to the ecosystem. Leopards are apex predators and help control the population of their prey. The loss of these animals can lead to catastrophic consequences and imbalance in the ecosystem.

Conservation efforts are aimed at protecting Amur leopard habitats, ensuring that people living near these areas coexist peacefully with the leopards. Solutions to this problem include strict enforcement of anti-poaching laws and initiatives to reduce climate change.

But conservation efforts are not just a matter of protecting endangered species - they're also important for our own wellbeing. For example, the protection of these endangered wildlife can go hand-in-hand with the protection of their ecosystems. These initiatives can lead to the preservation of natural habitats, which in turn ensure that we have clean air, water, and fertile soils.

In conclusion, Amur leopards are endangered because of habitat loss, poaching, and climate change. Despite their precarious situation, there's still hope for these majestic animals. By working together, we can protect their habitats, prevent poaching, and reduce the impact of climate change. Doing so ensures that the Amur leopard, and the many other species that call our planet home, can be cherished for generations to come.

Hawksbill sea turtles:

Hawksbill sea turtles, or Eretmochelys imbricata, are one of the world's most beautiful and unique species of sea turtles. They are named for their narrow, pointed beaks that look like a bird of prey, and for their intricate and colorful shells. These magnificent creatures are found mostly in tropical and subtropical waters all over the world.

Unfortunately, Hawksbill sea turtles are one of the most critically endangered species on the planet. There are many reasons for this, but most of them come down to humans and the impact we have on the world around us.

One of the main reasons why these turtles are in danger is due to habitat loss and destruction. As human populations continue to grow, we build more and more coastal developments that take over the nesting and feeding habitats of sea turtles. Hawksbill sea turtles typically lay their eggs on sandy beaches and then the hatchlings make their way to the ocean. When these places are destroyed or damaged, it becomes much harder for these creatures to survive and reproduce.

In addition to habitat loss, Hawksbill sea turtles are also threatened by hunting and fishing. Some cultures around the world hunt these turtles for their meat, eggs, and their beautiful shells. In some places, poachers will even steal eggs from nests, which makes it even harder for baby turtles to survive.

Another big problem for these sea turtles is pollution. Plastic pollution is one of the biggest threats to the survival of not just these turtles but many marine species. Hawksbill sea turtles are known to mistake plastic bags, straws, and other debris for jellyfish, which are a favorite food of theirs. Eating plastic can make them very sick, and in severe cases, it can kill them.

Finally, climate change is starting to have a significant impact on the survival of these turtles. As the planet continues to warm, the oceans are also getting warmer. This can change the patterns of where turtles lay their eggs and where they find their food. Rising sea levels caused by melting glaciers and ice caps also threaten the turtle's nesting areas.

All of these challenges make it very hard for Hawksbill sea turtles to survive in the wild. While there are many conservation efforts underway to help protect these animals, including laws that make it illegal to hunt these turtles or trade their shells, it's up to everyone to do their part to help preserve these magnificent creatures for the future

Mountain Gorillas:

Mountain gorillas, also known as Gorilla beringei beringei, are one of the world's rarest species of gorilla. Native to the forests and mountains in the borders of Rwanda,

Uganda, and the Democratic Republic of Congo, these majestic creatures are critically endangered with only around 1,063 left in the wild. Unfortunately, the reason for their precarious status is the impact of humans on their habitat.

One of the primary reasons why mountain gorillas are endangered is due to habitat loss and destruction. People in the area have been cutting down trees to clear land for farming, causing a reduction in the size of the forests where the gorillas live. This makes it harder for the gorillas to find food and resources, leading to lower population rates.

Another significant problem is poaching - the illegal hunting of these gorillas. While most forms of poaching are for meat, in the case of mountain gorillas, it is part of a deceptive trade that is driven by beliefs and superstitions. Some of these gorillas are captured for sale as pets or trade in exotic markets. Parts of these gorillas, such as their skulls and hands, are also taken for their perceived magical properties.

Diseases also put mountain gorillas at risk of extinction. They can catch illnesses from humans like colds and flu, which can be fatal. This is a severe problem for these primates in areas where tourists come to visit the gorillas. The people that visit the mountain gorillas are instructed to stay at least seven meters away at all times to avoid contamination or any cross-species transmission.

Climate change is another growing concern for these endangered animals. Change in weather patterns like a rise in temperatures, disturbance in rainfall pattern, and weather disasters threaten the mountain gorillas' food sources and habitats.

Many organizations and scientists work hard to protect these gorillas, but it will require a combined effort of several critical measures. Preventing deforestation, controlling hunting and poaching, reducing contact between gorillas and humans, and providing sufficient resources and protection of outdoor areas where these gorillas reside are essential.

In conclusion, the future of mountain gorillas lies in our hands. We must work together to address the various threats facing these majestic creatures, such as habitat destruction, poaching, and climate change. By taking action and supporting conservation efforts, we can help ensure that the mountain gorillas remain a living icon for future generations.

Giant Pandas:

Giant pandas are some of the most beloved and fascinating creatures on our planet. These cute and cuddly creatures are native to China's forested central highlands. Yet, these gentle giants are endangered, with only 1,864 still living in the wild. Unfortunately, most of the reasons for this can be attributed to humans.

One of the primary reasons giant pandas are endangered is due to habitat loss. As the population in China increases, more land gets cleared for agriculture or development, resulting in the displacement of these pandas. As a result, natural habitats are reduced by deforestation, which destroys their primary food source, bamboo. Giant pandas have a specialized digestive tract that can only digest bamboo shoots, making it harder for them to survive when this food source is scarce.

Another big problem for these pandas is hunting. People used to hunt pandas for their fur, and some also believed that the pandas' body parts had medicinal properties. Collecting pandas for use in zoos and entertainment parks also put immense pressure on the wild population.

Diseases also pose a significant threat to giant pandas. They are uniquely susceptible to many viral, bacterial, and parasitic diseases that cross the species barrier from other species. Pandas can also acquire diseases from humans who come into contact with them.

Finally, global warming is another problem for giant panda populations. The changing climate affects not only the bamboo that pandas eat but also causes other climatic changes such as natural disasters such as droughts, wildfires, and floods.

In conclusion, giant pandas are facing significant threats that are mostly human-made. Urbanization and deforestation, hunting and poaching, diseases, and global warming have all contributed to the decline in giant panda populations. Efforts to protect these amazing creatures, including forest conservation programs, biomedical research, and education programs, have helped stabilize the declining population. It is crucial to keep fighting for the well-being and safety of these captivating creatures to ensure future generations can appreciate their presence in the wild.

North Atlantic right whales:

North Atlantic right whales are a unique species of whale that is native to the Atlantic Ocean. Unfortunately, they are one of the most critically endangered whales on our planet, with only approximately 400 remaining in the wild. There are many reasons why these magnificent creatures are facing extinction. Out of these, most of them are human-driven.

One of the significant issues that have led to the endangered status of North Atlantic right whales is illegal hunting. Historically, these whales were almost hunted to extinction for their meat, bones, and blubber. Even though hunting these whales became illegal in the 1930s, their populations have been slow to recover.

Entanglement in fishing gear is another significant problem that affects North Atlantic right whales. These whales often get caught in nets and lines that are used by commercial fishermen. When they get caught in the gear, the lines become wrapped tightly around the whale, causing severe or even life-threatening injuries that can lead to death by starvation or suffocation.

Diseases are another primary challenge for North Atlantic right whales. These animals are especially susceptible to diseases and infections, which can spread through their communities very rapidly. New diseases that come from other species or interruptions in the food source they sustain on can significantly impact the population of the North Atlantic right whale.

Finally, climate change has become an increasingly significant threat faced by North Atlantic right whales. Rising water temperatures and acidity levels have caused significant disruptions to the whales' food supply, negatively impacting the survival of these magnificent creatures.

In conclusion, North Atlantic right whales are facing extinction due to multiple reasons, including overhunting, entanglement in fishing gear, disease, and climate change. To save these amazing creatures, it is vital that we take significant conservation efforts like reducing ship strikes, improving fishing gear to reduce entanglement, and restoring their habitats. Continued efforts can lead to protecting this wonderful species and preserving it for future generations.

Leatherback sea turtles:

Leatherback sea turtles are an incredible species that have existed on our oceans for over a hundred million years. Sadly, the population of these majestic creatures is in danger of extinction, and human activities have led to their decline.

The primary reason for the endangerment of leatherback sea turtles is habitat loss. These magnificent creatures tend to nest on remote, sandy beaches that are gradually being destroyed and transformed because of human activities like urbanization, tourism, and development. As a result, there are fewer and fewer beaches available for them to nest, leading to a decrease in the population of leatherback sea turtles.

Another significant issue for leatherback sea turtles is illegal hunting. In some parts of the world, these creatures are hunted for their meat, eggs, and shells, which are considered delicacies or used for traditional customs. Hunting has led to a significant decline in the population of the turtles, despite laws to prohibit this activity.

Pollution is another contributing factor to the endangerment of leatherback sea turtles. The oceans and seas are becoming increasingly polluted, with plastic bags, debris, and other contaminants, which the turtles often mistake for food. This pollution can lead to blockages of the turtles' digestive tract, causing injuries, and even death.

Large fishing gear, such as longlines, pose another threat to leatherback sea turtles. These lines can entangle the turtles, causing severe injuries or death. Additionally, the accidental capture of these turtles in fishing gear severely affects their survival rate.

Climate change is also having a significant impact on the leatherback sea turtle's population. The warming of the oceans leads to changes in plant and animal life, ultimately affecting the turtles' food source and habitat, thereby increasing their vulnerability.

In conclusion, the population of leatherback sea turtles is facing endangerment due to several human-related issues. To save them, we need to implement conservation efforts like the protection of nesting beaches, stricter regulations and enforcement against poaching, reduction of plastic pollution, and development of technologies that will reduce the number of accidental captures in fishing gear. By working together to protect these incredible creatures, we can ensure that future generations will continue to enjoy their presence in our oceans.

North Atlantic right whales are a species of whale that call the Atlantic Ocean their home. Unfortunately, they are also one of the most endangered whales on the planet, with only about 400 remaining in the wild.

There are many reasons why these magnificent creatures are in danger, and most of them are caused by human actions. For example, hunting used to be a significant threat to North Atlantic right whales. In the past, people hunted these whales for their blubber, meat, and bones almost to the point of extinction. Although hunting them became illegal in the 1930s, their populations have been slow to recover.

Another significant problem for North Atlantic right whales is entanglement in fishing gear. These whales can get trapped in nets and fishing lines that are used by commercial fishermen, which can cause serious or even life-threatening injuries. If the gear is wrapped too tightly around the whale, it can lead to drowning, suffocation, or starvation.

Diseases are also a major problem for North Atlantic right whales. These animals are particularly susceptible to diseases and infections, which can spread through their communities very rapidly. New diseases that come from other species or disruptions in the food cycle they rely on can significantly impact the population of North Atlantic right whale.

Finally, climate change is also having an impact on North Atlantic right whales. Rising water temperatures and ocean acidity levels have caused disruptions to the whales' food supply, which can negatively impact their survival. These changes to their environment can make it harder for them to find food and make it more difficult for them to reproduce.

In conclusion, North Atlantic right whales are endangered for multiple reasons, including overhunting, entanglement in fishing gear, disease, and climate change. However, conservation efforts can help ensure the survival of these magnificent creatures. For example, reducing ship strikes, improving fishing gear to reduce entanglement, and restoring their habitats can all have a positive impact on the whale's chances of survival. With continued effort, future generations can experience and appreciate the beauty of these amazing creatures.

CHAPTER 6

GOODNIGHT TO THE FLOWERS

Welcome to the enchanting world of flowers! In this chapter, we'll be exploring what makes flowers so magnificent - not just their beauty, but also their cultural meanings, fascinating new uses, and why preserving our natural resources is more important now than ever.

Flowers are one of the most fascinating wonders of the natural world. Of course, it's hard not to be captivated by their vibrant hues and sweet scents, but did you know that flowers also have cultural significance and meanings attached to them? Across different cultures, certain flowers hold particular symbolic meanings that have been passed down through generations. It's incredible to think how something as delicate as a flower can hold so much history and significance.

Flowers are also useful in some surprising ways, beyond just making the world a more beautiful place. Take perfumes, for example - did you know that some of the most expensive perfumes in the world are made with flower extracts? Flowers also have a long history of use in medicine, with many cultures around the world using floral remedies to alleviate common ailments. As science continues to explore the potential of flower-based compounds, we're likely to discover even more uses for these magnificent botanicals.

Gardening is another way to appreciate the beauty of flowers. Whether you have a large garden or just a few pots on your windowsill, cultivating flowers can bring a sense of calm and connection with the natural world. But with global climate change on the rise, it's more important than ever to take steps to conserve our natural resources. By becoming more mindful about our use of water, soil, and other resources, we can work together to ensure that natural beauty like flowers continues to thrive in the future.

So join us as we explore the world of flowers - their beauty

Flowers have a magnetic appeal that fascinates and inspires people. Their unique colors, patterns, scents, and textures make them a timeless symbol of natural beauty. But did you know that the cultural significance of flowers goes far beyond their beauty? Different countries and cultures across the world assign meanings to different types of flowers, making them not only a remarkable aspect of natural beauty but also a communicative and expressive tool.

In ancient times, giving flowers was a common practice for people to express their emotions, such as love, sympathy, and gratitude. And this practice has remained for centuries. The language of flowers, known as floriography, emerged during the Victorian era, where people used flowers to send messages to their loved ones silently.

Today, we still use flowers to communicate our sentiments on different occasions. People still give red roses to their loved one to express their love and affection and white roses to symbolize purity, innocence, and sympathy.

But it's not just our Western culture that associates symbolic meanings with flowers! In Japan, the cherry blossom, or Sakura, has great cultural importance and influence. It signifies the beginning of spring and the renewal of life. During the celebrations that welcome this season, people have picnics under the cherry blossom trees, taking pictures and admiring the beauty of the nature.

Similarly, in India, marigolds have a sacred meaning, representing good fortune, happiness, and prosperity. Indian people even decorate their homes and vehicles with marigold garlands during festivities and celebrations.

The cultural significance of flowers stretches beyond just serving as ornamental pieces. They also commonly feature in traditional art such as music, literature, and painting. Writers and poets often use flowers as symbols in their works, such as Shakespeare's use of roses as a symbol of love in his works. As well, many renowned musicians, such as Louis Armstrong with his song "What A Wonderful World," sang about the beauty of flowers in their songs, making reference to the blossoming flora's beauty.

In conclusion, flowers bring not just joy and peace to our hearts, but they also hold natural and cultural meanings that differ and merge from one culture to another. Whether it's associating love with the red rose or spirituality with the cherry blossom, the symbolic power of flowers continues to fascinate and hold significance throughout the world.

Flowers have been used for medicinal purposes for centuries. From Egypt to Greece and beyond, people have discovered the healing powers of flowers. One of the most well-known medicinal flowers is echinacea, known for its antiviral properties and used to boost the immune system to prevent colds and respiratory infections. Another well-known flower is chamomile, which has a calming effect on the body and promotes restful sleep, making it a popular ingredient in teas and other natural remedies.

Moreover, Some other flowers, like hibiscus, can offer several health benefits, such as lowering blood pressure and supporting liver function, thanks to their antioxidant properties. Peony is also becoming popular as a natural pain-relieving agent for women with menstrual cramps. In addition, the humble dandelion flower has several health benefits like relieving digestive issues and even skin problems.

The use of flowers doesn't just stop at traditional medicine. Modern medicine also uses flower extracts to create powerful drugs that can cure various illnesses. For example, aspirin, which is widely used as a pain-reliever in modern medicine, is derived from the bark of the willow tree. Similarly, Taxol, a drug used to treat some types of cancer, comes from the Pacific Yew tree's bark.

Flowers also play an important role in the beauty industry. Many beauty and skincare products have flower-based ingredients, including lotions, creams, and perfumes. Jasmine, for example, is a popular flower that's been used for centuries in perfumes to create a seductive and alluring aroma. Meanwhile, lavender is also used in aromatherapy to promote relaxation and reduce anxiety.

Finally, some flowers are even edible! Not only do they add visual appeal to dishes, but they can also provide extra flavor and nutrition. Chrysanthemums, for example, are a popular flower used in Asia to make tea, thought to help prevent soreness and even boost the immune system. Nasturtiums are also used in cooking to add a spicy flavor to salads and other dishes.

In conclusion, flowers are anything but just pretty decorations! From traditional medicine to modern medicine, beauty products and even food, flowers have proven themselves to be multi-talented and essential. It's amazing to see how something so beautiful can also have so many practical uses!

Perfumes have been made for thousands of years, and flowers are a key ingredient in creating beautiful fragrances. The scent of flowers can range from gentle and sweet to pungent and unmistakable, allowing for a wide variety of perfume creations. Let's take a deeper look at some of the flowers used in perfumes.

The smell of roses is quintessential when it comes to fragrances. The perfume industry often uses rose essential oil, which is made by distilling petals in water. The result is an oil that has a sweet, floral scent that's warm and comforting. Roses are often used in perfumes that are feminine and classic, making them a popular choice for many perfume concoctions.

Jasmine is another essential oil used in perfumes. Its sweet and intoxicating fragrance is sensual and exotic, and often used to create long-lasting fragrances. Jasmine essential oil is produced in a similar way to the rose, and when blended with other flowery or fruity scents, it has been known to create an unforgettable aroma.

Lavender, with its soothing and calming properties, is also used in perfumery. The aroma is subtle and sweet, and blends perfectly with other floral or herbal scents. Lavender is often used in perfumes that are light and refreshing, making them perfect to wear during the day.

Lily of the valley is another flower that's popular in perfumery. The scent of this flower is refreshing and has a soft, delicate, and almost powdery finish. Lily of the valley is often used as a middle note in perfumes and can add depth and dimension to other floral fragrances.

Ylang-ylang is another beloved flower used in perfumes. Its sweet, exotic bouquet has a sensual quality that appeals to many. Ylang-ylang essential oil is often blended with other ingredients to create a scent that's both deep and fresh. When used in perfumes, it can create an unforgettable fragrance that commands attention.

Lastly, we cannot forget peonies. With their vibrant colors and lovely scent, peonies make the perfect flower in perfumery with their fresh, sweet, and airy fragrance.

In conclusion, the power of flowers in scent creation is undeniable. Their unique and irresistible fragrances have captured the hearts of the perfume industry for a long time. From the sweet and flagrant jasmine to the delicate and powdery lily of the valley, each flower offers different qualities and dimensions to the world of perfumes, making them a crucial ingredient in creating tantalizing scents. Enjoy the everlasting beauty of flowers in all their forms!

Gardening is one of the most rewarding and satisfying hobbies you can pick up. It's a creative outlet that allows you to grow your plants and engage with nature. The best part is, you don't have to be an expert to start. All you need is a love for plants and a willingness to learn.

The first thing you should consider is what kind of garden you want to create. There are different types of gardens, ranging from vegetable gardens to flower gardens. You can also create a themed garden, such as an herb garden or a butterfly garden. Different types of gardens have different methods and requirements, so take some time to research which one will suit your interests best.

Once you have an idea of what kind of garden you want to create, find a space in your yard that receives enough sunlight. Plants need sunlight, water, and air to grow, so make sure the area you choose allows for good air circulation. If you don't have a yard, don't worry – you can create a garden in pots or containers on your patio, balcony or windowsill.

The next step is to prepare the soil. Healthy soil is the foundation of a thriving garden. Soil should be rich in nutrients, well-draining, and have the right pH levels. You can improve the soil quality by adding compost or organic matter.

Once you have your garden plot set up and soil prepared, it's time to start planting. Choose plants that are suitable for your area's climate, soil type, and sunlight levels. You can obtain plant seeds and seedlings from local nurseries, garden centers, or online.

One thing to keep in mind is that growing plants takes time and patience. Some plants take longer to germinate and mature than others, so don't be discouraged if your garden doesn't look like the pictures right away. As you gain experience, you'll learn which plants thrive best in your growing environment, and you'll become skilled at taking care of them.

Caring for your plants includes watering them regularly, weeding, and fertilizing. Be sure to monitor your plants for pests and diseases, and take measures to prevent or treat them as soon as you spot a problem. Regular maintenance and care will help your garden thrive and be healthy.

In addition to the aesthetic benefits of gardening, there are many other rewards. Gardening can act as a form of therapy, helping to reduce stress levels and improve mental health. It can also be a fun activity to do with family and friends, and a great way to get some exercise outdoors.

Overall, gardening is an incredibly rewarding and fulfilling hobby that offers so many benefits, both for you and for the environment. With some planning and attention, anyone can create a beautiful and productive garden – no green thumb required!

Gardening can be a lot of fun, but it can also be challenging without the right tools. Fortunately, there are many tools out there designed specifically for gardening that can make your job easier and more efficient.

1. **Garden Gloves** - Essential for protecting your hands from thorns, blisters, and other injuries.

2. **Pruning Shears** - Used to trim away dead or damaged parts of plants, keeping them healthy and promoting growth.

3. **Trowel** - A small, handheld shovel that's useful for planting bulbs, digging small holes, and transplanting seedlings.

4. **Garden Rake** - Used to smooth soil, remove rocks, and level the ground before planting. The tines can also be used to break up clumps.

5. **Wheelbarrow** - Used to transport soil, compost, and plants around the garden. It's a great tool for transporting heavy items without having to carry them.

6. **Garden Pruner** - Used to cut back unwanted growth on bushes and trees. Can also be used to cut small branches and stems.

7. **Shovel** - A larger version of the trowel, great for digging holes, moving large amounts of soil, and transplanting larger plants.

8. **Watering Can or Hose** - Essential for keeping your garden hydrated and promoting plant growth.

9. **Hoe** - Used to remove weeds and to break up soil, making it easier to plant. The shape of the blade helps to slice through the soil with ease.

10. **Garden Fork** - Helpful for preparing soil, loosening compacted soil, and aerating the top layer of soil.

Additional tools such as kneeling pads, spraying bottles, and handheld seed spreaders can also be useful for specific tasks. When selecting gardening tools, it's important to invest in high-quality tools that will last for years. With the right tools, gardening can be a satisfying and enjoyable hobby that produces beautiful results. So put on your gloves, grab your tools, and start nurturing your garden!

Natural resources are anything that the planet provides us with, such as water, air, sunlight, minerals, forests, and oceans. They are the building blocks of life and are essential for our survival. However, human activities have put a tremendous strain on natural resources, and the need to conserve them has become increasingly important.

The conservation of natural resources is crucial for preserving biodiversity. Conserving natural resources helps protect the habitats and ecosystems of different plant and animal species, providing them with the necessary conditions to thrive. Biodiversity is essential to the survival of all living things, providing services like pollination, nutrient cycling, and water filtration.

Conservation of natural resources also helps maintain soil quality and prevent erosion. Soils are crucial for plant growth and play a vital role in carbon and water cycles. It is, therefore, important to maintain healthy soils through sustainable land management practices such as crop rotation, reduced tillage, and the use of cover crops.

Conservation is also critical for the preservation of air and water quality. Clean air and water are essential to human health. Human activities like pollution, deforestation, and carbon emissions all contribute to the depletion of natural resources and threaten the quality of our air and water. Conserving these resources is essential to protect human health and mitigate the impact of climate change.

Conservation of natural resources also supports sustainable development and economic growth. Sustainable practices such as renewable energy, energy efficiency, and sustainable agriculture are vital sources of economic growth while also reducing environmental impacts.

Another significant benefit of conservation is the resilience of ecosystems. By maintaining healthy ecosystems, we can help mitigate the impact of natural disasters like floods, storms, and droughts that are becoming more severe due to climate change.

Conservation of natural resources also ensures that future generations can enjoy and benefit from them. It is our responsibility to take care of the planet and provide a sustainable future for all. Education and awareness campaigns can help promote the importance of conservation, and policymakers can take strong measures to protect our natural resources.

In conclusion, natural resources are vital to our survival, and the conservation of these resources is crucial for future generations. Through sustainable practices and responsible resource use, we can conserve natural resources and create a healthier and sustainable future for all life on this planet.

In conclusion, this chapter has taken us on a journey through the world of flowers and highlighted the significance of preserving our natural resources. Flowers are a natural wonder that brings beauty and life to our surroundings, and their cultural meanings, fascinating new uses, and beneficial medicinal properties make them all the more enchanting.

From various cultures associating different flowers with symbolic meanings to the amazing uses found for them in perfumes, medicine, and food, flowers prove to be one of the most multi-talented and essential gifts of nature. The fact that something as delicate as a flower can hold so much history and significance is truly fascinating.

Furthermore, gardening is a wonderful way to appreciate the beauty of flowers and cultivate a connection with the natural world. Whether you have a large garden or just a few pots on a windowsill, gardening can provide a sense of calm and fulfillment. It's also an excellent way to experience the benefits of outdoor activities, exercise, and fresh air.

However, amidst all of these wonders, we must acknowledge the importance of responsible use of resources and conservation. Our planet is facing a multitude of environmental challenges, and we must work together to ensure that our natural resources are preserved for generations to come. By becoming more mindful of our water, soil, and other resource usage, we can create a healthier future for our planet and the natural beauty of flowers.

Preserving our natural resources is crucial for sustaining biodiversity, maintaining soil quality, protecting air and water quality, supporting sustainable development and economic growth, and creating resilient ecosystems that can better withstand natural disasters and climate change.

To conclude, the world of flowers is one of beauty and wonder, but it also reminds us of the importance of preserving and protecting our natural resources. By being conscious of our resource use and supporting sustainable practices, we can help ensure a future that is both healthy and beautiful for all.

■■

CHAPTER 7

CONCLUSION

At a time when we're increasingly aware of the climate crisis and the impact of human activities on the planet, this book reminds us of the beauty and wonder of the natural world and prompts us to think deeply about the importance of conserving it. Each chapter explored a different natural wonder, from sunsets and stars to animals and flowers, and helped us gain deeper insights into their significance from different cultural perspectives.

In the first chapter, we learned about the beauty of sunsets and how different cultures have their unique ways of bidding farewell to the sun each day. The second chapter introduced us to the constellations and the magic of stargazing, and reminded us of how we are all connected through the universal language of the stars. In chapter three, we dove into the oceans and learned about the importance of marine life conservation and how we can help protect the rich diversity of marine ecosystems.

Chapter four brought us into the world's forests, highlighting their beauty and importance as habitats for countless animal species and sources of clean air and water. However, we also confront the challenges of deforestation and the urgent need for reforestation to protect the planet's biodiversity. As we move through the fifth chapter, we're introduced to the diverse range of animals that call the planet home, and the urgent need for conservation efforts to protect endangered species.

Finally, we come to chapter six and the beauty of flowers. We learned how different cultures use flowers as powerful symbols, and the ways in which flowers play important roles in medicine, perfumes, and other essential elements of our lives. This chapter also emphasized the importance of natural resources and gardening in conserving our planet's beauty.

Taken together, the chapters of this book aim to inspire us to say goodnight to the Earth with a sense of gratitude, respect, and responsibility. By understanding the cultural and symbolic significance of each natural wonder, readers can appreciate and respect the natural world more fully, recognize the cultural richness of the planet's biodiversity, and become agents of change who work to protect these wonders for future generations. Our world is a place of incredible beauty and creativity, and it's up to each of us to play our part in safeguarding it. Let's do so with open hearts and a deep commitment to protecting the wonder and beauty of our shared home.

As we wind down at night and prepare for bed, it's important to take a moment to reflect on the interconnectedness of the world around us. Through our daily routines, it's easy to forget the significance of the natural world that keeps us alive and thriving. Hence, it's essential to reinforce the importance of taking care of the Earth and appreciating its beauty - even at bedtime.

Our planet is familiar to us, yet consistently leaves us awestruck. Its vastness, complexity, and interdependence are what make it a marvel to behold. Yet, as the world's population grows, urbanizes, and industrializes, so too do the challenges facing the environment. The deteriorating air quality, contaminated water resources, and the loss of biodiversity are just a few examples of the consequences the planet faces due to irresponsible human action. It is our responsibility as inhabitants of Earth to take care of our planet to ensure its longevity and our survival.

Fortunately, there are many ways we can champion the cause of environmental protection. One of the simplest is to practice resource conservation and reduce waste. This means we should be mindful of not overusing water, we should recycle, and conserve energy to prevent the further depletion of natural resources. In addition, we can participate in causes or charities that support conservation efforts. These are just the starting steps on the path to protecting the planet.

As we wind down and prepare our minds to drift off to sleep, we can take a moment to appreciate the beauty of the world around us. The night sky, the gentle breeze on our skin, the sound of rustling wind amid trees - all these natural wonders offer a deep, calming sense of peace. By taking time to observe and appreciate these wonders that surround us, we can foster a deeper sense of appreciation, respect, and connection to the planet.

Another way to appreciate the natural world is through learning about different natural wonders. Our planet offers an endless variety of beauty and wonder, from the Aurora Borealis to the vast coral reefs and deep-water trenches. We must take time to learn and understand their importance and the need to protect them for future generations.

In conclusion, taking care of the Earth and appreciating its beauty is essential in every aspect of our life. Amidst our daily routines, it's easy to overlook the significance of the environment and its contribution towards our survival. By cultivating a sense of responsibility and appreciation for the planet, we can protect and appreciate all that the world has to offer, even at bedtime.

Help Us Share Your Thoughts!

Dear Reader,

Thank you for choosing to read our book. We hope you enjoyed the journey through its pages and that it left a positive impact on your life. As an independent author, reviews from readers like you are incredibly valuable in helping us reach a wider audience and improve our craft.

If you enjoyed our book, we kindly ask for a moment of your time to leave an honest review on Amazon. Your feedback can make a world of difference by providing potential readers with insight into the book's content and your personal experience.

To leave a review, simply follow these easy steps:

Visit the Amazon page where you bought the book.

Scroll down to the "Customer Reviews" section.

Click on the "Write a customer review" button.

Share your thoughts, opinions, and overall impression of the book.

Click "Submit" to post your review.

Your review doesn't have to be lengthy or complicated—just a few lines expressing your genuine thoughts would be immensely appreciated. We value your feedback and take it to heart, using it to shape our future work and create more content that resonates with readers like you.

By leaving a review, you are not only supporting us as authors but also helping other readers discover this book. Your voice matters, and your words have the power to inspire others to embark on this literary journey.

We genuinely appreciate your time and willingness to share your thoughts. Thank you for being an essential part of our author journey.

GOODNIGHT WORLD: A TOUR OF THE EARTH'S WONDERS